THE DAY'S RATION

THE DAY'S RANSOM

Gilles Ortlieb
THE DAY'S RATION
SELECTED POEMS

Translated by Patrick McGuinness
& Stephen Romer

Introduced by Sean O'Brien

Published by Arc Publications,
Nanholme Mill, Shaw Wood Road
Todmorden OL14 6DA, UK
www.arcpublications.co.uk

Copyright: © Gilles Ortlieb, 2023
Copyright: © Editions Gallimard, 2002

Translation copyright © Patrick McGuinness &
Stephen Romer, 2023
Introduction copyright © Sean O'Brien, 2023
Afterword copyright © Patrick McGuinness &
Stephen Romer, 2023
Copyright in the present edition © Arc Publications, 2023

978 1911469 42 1 (pbk)

Design by Tony Ward
Printed in Great Britain by T.J. Books Ltd,
Padstow, Cornwall

Cover illustration © Gilles Ortlieb

This book is in copyright. Subject to statutory exception and to provision of relevant collective licensing agreements, no reproduction of any part of this book may take place without the written permission of Arc Publications.

**Arc Publications 'Visible Poets' series
Series Editor: Jean Boase-Beier**

CONTENTS

Series Editor's Note / 9
Introduction / 11

Brouillard journalier / Logbook of Days

16 / 'Un toit de zinc mis à nu...' • 'A zinc roof laid bare...' / 17
18 / 'Absurde de s'obstiner à aller ainsi...' • 'Absurd to trudge on like this...' / 19
20 / 'À nouveau la chasse balancée par les rues...' • 'Once again, it's the sardonic but stubborn...' / 21
22 / 'Que la rue, surtout, soit mon habitante...' • 'So let the street be my addiction...' / 23
24 / 'Les deux plis de l'eau contre la pile d'un pont...' • 'The two crests of water against the pillar of a bridge...' / 25
26 / 'Poussière d'or, oui, par quel rare soupirail?...' • 'Gold dust, coming from the odd basement window...' / 27
28 / 'Le passant attardé sur les places ignore...' • 'The passer-by, lingering late in the squares...' / 29
30 / 'Pensées de nuit, poignée de cailloux au puits...' • 'Night thoughts, handful of pebbles down a well...' / 31

Liasse de l'Est / East of Here

32 / Trois miniatures • Three Miniatures / 33
34 / Compagnies • Companies / 35
36 / Traversées • Crossings / 37
38 / Wagon de queue • Rear Carriage / 39
40 / Contretemps • Setback / 41
42 / Cafés de la frontière • Frontier Cafés / 43
44 / Dernière promenade • Final Stroll / 45
46 / 'Neige à Thionville, lumières petites, lumières...' • 'Snow in Thionville, small lights, lights...' / 47

48 / 'La brume a dissimulé la • 'The mist has concealed the
  brume…'   mist…' / 49
50 / 'Petite ville aux reflets de • 'Small town with its gleams of
  houille et d'étain…'   coal and tin…' / 51
52 / Ballast courant • Sleeper Gravel / 53
54 / Café de l'Usine • Café de l'Usine / 55
56 / Février • February / 57
58 / Pavillon des incurables • Hospice Wing / 59

Sous le crible / Under the Sieve

62 / Les mauvaises soirées • The Bad Evenings / 63
64 / Un geste • A Movement / 65
66 / Noël à Ithaque • Christmas on Ithaca / 67
68 / Encore • Once Again / 69
70 / Exit • Exit / 71
72 / 3h56 • 3.56 a.m. / 73
74 / La matinée des choses • The Morning of Insignificant
  insignifiantes   Things / 75
76 / En train, pour changer • On the Train (for a change) / 77
78 / Cela • It / 79
80 / Ode (pour traverser les • Ode (for getting through the
  jours sans maugréer)   days without whinging) / 81

Décembres / Decembers

82 / 'Voici plusieurs jours, en • 'For several days now, in
  somme…'   short…' / 83
84 / 'Décembre, mois entre tous • 'December, month the most
  malcommode…'   awkward of all…' / 85
86 / 'Veille de veille de Noël • 'Antepenultimate day before
  dans l'Est…'   Christmas in the East…' / 87
88 / 'Par la fenêtre un petit • 'Through the window a little
  homme en cache-col…'   man in a bronze scarf…' / 89
90 / 'Arrière-cour en hiver, • 'A closed courtyard in winter,
  avec fumées montant…'   smoke climbing…' / 91
92 / 'La saison se désincarcère • 'Grudgingly, the season cuts free
  de la saison, à reculons…'   from the season…' / 93

Le train des jours / Days Going By

94 / Grues et fumées • Cranes and Smoke / 95
98 / Mi-août ferroviaire • Entrainings, mid-August / 99
100 / 'Marmande, 22h30 : train • '22.30, Marmande: the train for
annoncé avec un retard...' Agen, Montauban...' / 101
102 / 'Une fois à bord du train • 'Safe aboard the train, no sooner
enfin arrivé...' arrived...' / 103

Notes in Transit / 105

Removals / 109

Notes in February / 113

Afterword / 115

Acknowledgements / 120

Biographical Notes / 121

SERIES EDITOR'S NOTE

The 'Visible Poets' series was established in 2000, and set out to challenge the view that translated poetry could or should be read without regard to the process of translation it had undergone. Since then, things have moved on. Today there is more translated poetry available and more debate on its nature, its status, and its relation to its original. We know that translated poetry is neither English poetry that has mysteriously arisen from a hidden foreign source, nor is it foreign poetry that has silently rewritten itself in English. We are more aware that translation lies at the heart of all our cultural exchange; without it, we must remain artistically and intellectually insular.

One of the aims of the series was, and still is, to enrich our poetry with the very best work that has appeared elsewhere in the world. And the poetry-reading public is now more aware than it was at the start of this century that translation cannot simply be done by anyone with two languages. The translation of poetry is a creative act, and translated poetry stands or falls on the strength of the poet-translator's art. For this reason 'Visible Poets' publishes only the work of the best translators, and gives each of them space, in a Preface, to talk about the trials and pleasures of their work.

From the start, 'Visible Poets' books have been bilingual. Many readers will not speak the languages of the original poetry but they, too, are invited to compare the look and shape of the English poems with the originals. Those who can are encouraged to read both. Translation and original are presented side-by-side because translations do not displace the originals; they shed new light on them and are in turn themselves illuminated by the presence of their source poems. By drawing the readers' attention to the act of translation itself, it is the aim of these books to make the work of both the original poets and their translators more visible.

Jean Boase-Beier

INTRODUCTION

'One is always nearer by not keeping still.' So states the famous closing line of 'On the Move', Thom Gunn's poem about a motorcycle gang. The restlessness apparent in Gilles Ortlieb's poems of trains, hotels and solitary evenings might seem to be of the same order. But whereas the bikers have made an existential choice – to exercise the will through perpetual movement, without ascribing meaning to the landscape through which they travel – Ortlieb's poems are preoccupied with an earlier dilemma: is the world a mirror or a lamp? Do we simply visit our preoccupations on our surroundings, or is there an underlying correspondence between one more glum hotel room and the mind that contemplates it? Is there something in here or out there to understand? And might we be subject to judgement, as Larkin tentatively suggests in 'Mr Bleaney', so that the fact of being here may mean that we deserve no better?

A biographical note on Gilles Ortlieb indicates someone to whom movement is a given. Born in Morocco in 1953, Ortlieb studied at the Sorbonne, travelled in the Mediterranean and developed an enduring love of Greek culture, publishing a selection of translations of Cavafy, Seferis, and others. For some twenty years he worked at the European Translation agency, located in Luxembourg. The tiny polyglot Grand Duchy, bordering France, Belgium and Germany, is easily overlooked. Like other financial centres it practises a quiet discretion. The suspicion remains, unfairly, that it is not quite a place in its own right but an agreement between borders, somewhere existing as it were in translation. Such an ambiguous state seems an obvious location for Ortlieb. From there, he himself is physically 'translated', or translates himself, across Europe, much of the time by rail, which offers specific privileges to the imagination. For example, his 'home' landscape, explored in collections including *Meuse Metal, etc.* (2005) is the heavy industrial and mining region, long in decline, in which the borders of Belgium, Luxembourg and France meet, the kind of place the founders of the EU had in mind at the end of the Second World War, when coal was still almost king. On the edge of Volmerange-les-Mines,

'the *No Man's Land* stands
face to face with *L'Entre-Deux*, a former customs hut
now converted into a chip stall on the other side
of the country road: the frontier is close by,
barely two hundred metres
and ten years away.'
(*Place au cirque*, 2002)

The magnetism of such bleak and economically posthumous settings is irresistible: the poet relaxes; so does the place. The poet sees a kind of Beckettian comedy; the place, while appearing to do nothing, turns its irony on the poet. It compels, it exhausts, it seduces. It shows the poet, in the words of Wallace Stevens, 'nothing that is not there and the nothing that is,' a climate where he neither arrives nor departs. Ortlieb has found a post-industrial equivalent of Rodenbach's Bruges-la-Morte.

So let the street be my addiction,
the acrid vapours over the termini,
the intermittent spitting of the storm:
the summer's allotment, and slow afternoons
where I walk, trapped in a cipher of footsteps,

to watch the barges disappear under the arches
and smoke my endless, thin cigarettes
to bring these syllables to the surface.
(*Brouillard Journalier*, 1984)

As this beautifully measured and typically brief poem indicates, liking or not liking such places is irrelevant: the imagination must reach its own resigned, uneasy accommodation.

He travels lightest who travels alone. The railways, rooms and evening walks that characterize much of Ortlieb's poetry offer no companionship: nor do the poems seem to seek the consolation of company, conversation or sex. In 'Companies', the landscape is seen running away from the train that passes through it:

running – away from what? From the frost,
the salt, the leaves imprisoned in iron
water, spectres of the cold, and of the self.
(*Sous le crible*, 2008)

The striking Baudelairean conclusion, unembarrassed by plainly stating the terms of the *correspondance*, recognizes the self as a feature of the depersonalized process of travel: the self with no place, perhaps with no self outwith the superior vagrancy of gainful employment. The condition recalls Poe's obsessive flâneur in 'The Man of the Crowd', who lives, if he lives at all, on the nourishment of crowds as he makes his frenzied, unsleeping way through the city.

In one sense the astonishing, revelatory 'Rear Carriage' (*Sous le crible*) affirms the beauty of the tracks themselves:

a lasting idyll this, done in charcoal, between
the viaducts, the bridges and the distances,
a smudged-in black.

The poem also shows us a world engineered to perfection, a mechanism on the brink of the supernatural, a composition where a single track with a pair of rails divides and re-divides to form the great chord of tracks that emerges as the city approaches and then once more 'retract[s] into [a] binary and hypnotic scheme' as the train departs. The poem resembles a *coup de cinéma* like the process shot from the rear of the train in Hitchcock's *The Lady Vanishes* or the slow gliding of the tracks out of the darkness and under the train at the opening of Von Trier's *Europa*. Ortlieb arrives at a form of the industrial sublime. But these lines do not signal an exit from the labyrinth. It will have reset itself by the time he next looks up and leaves the train in a wintry city at night, where a few residents hurry home to eat and the traveller's prospects are few. If these travels reveal the consolations of solitude, they also show their limitations – another day, another night, another room. There's a laconic brinkmanship to this. Given these conditions of extreme marginality, it might make sense to fall silent. What can there be to add? The affinity with Cavafy becomes clear. Something will present itself. There will be a notebook entry to revisit later, as Ortlieb indicates in his sequence 'Decembers': 'this quasi- / appeasement… at first light, / emerging from the close dark with its / unsteady currents into a dawn swept by lights, / streetlamps, living streets…' For all their dissatisfaction, the poems reveal a stubborn and very appealing imaginative resilience – almost a relish of a besetting discouragement, exemplified in 'A Movement' (*Place au cirque*, 2002):

A MOVEMENT

tiny and venerable, consists in running the back of the spoon
over and against the edge of the plate or soup-bowl
to stop it from dripping on its journey to the mouth;
a rite, faintly audible, and worn through by long
practice in over or under-lit narrow kitchens,
within the confines of a one-eyed village or a vertical
suburb, left to themselves; an action that belongs
to a lonely man or woman, under a bare bulb, thoughts slowed,
returning to stumble against the obstacle of thinking
when the hand, following the curve, drops a little,
right at the end, as it re-acknowledges existence.

The poem is a single extended sentence of classical lucidity and Proustian relish (that word again) whose wry humour depends on never letting on that this degree of attention, close to madness, also serves to dignify its theme. In a sense this is the obverse of the playfulness of Francis Ponge's poems, but Ortlieb's forensic care is also a sign of human sympathy. If nothing else, these glimpsed and unknowable fellow travellers in time have solitude in common. And from the point of view of poetics, Ortlieb also shows how very far realism is from exhausting its resources.

Sean O'Brien

Brouillard journalier

Un toit de zinc mis à nu
dans l'échancrure des neiges trouées :
les premiers élans, l'amertume recouvrée
et peiner à peupler les rues,
les quais, les arbres raides.
Il n'y a pas si longtemps,
un fifre bousculait les cathédrales
– hiver entrevu, dans les mille
déclins de la pensée. Et puis le baiser
fatigué du lierre contre les eaux,
la lumière jetée sur les ponts
et nous tous, là, habitants des faubourgs,
revenants des saisons apprises.

Logbook of Days

A zinc roof laid bare
through the broken, dented snow:
first inklings, bitterness recouped,
the streets still untempting
and the quayside, stiffened trees.
Not so long ago
a penny whistle could topple cathedrals
– winter glimpsed, through the thousand
declensions of thought. And the weary kiss
that ivy lays upon the waters,
light thrown up on the bridges
and on all of us, from the poorer quarters,
veterans of seasons past.

Absurde de s'obstiner à aller ainsi
contre le vent coulis des hivers immobiles.
On détale vite, par expérience,
dès que les pas s'enferment sous des teintures d'orage.
Il reste un couteau de poche, pour les vivres du jour
papiers épars tout autour du dormeur
et la certitude retrouvée, au réveil,
que rien ne pourra l'acquitter de la longue fuite.

Absurd to trudge on like this
against the oozing wind of fixed
winters. Experience teaches you to scarper quick
when your steps freeze under rags of storm.
There's a pocket knife, for the day's rations,
papers scattered round the sleeper and the certitude
– recognized on waking –
nothing will absolve him from his headlong flight.

À nouveau, la chasse balancée par les rues
narquoise, obstinée. Un crayon, le tabac
et le livre, argenterie nécessaire
jusqu'à la lassitude d'écrire,
pour la seule compagnie des vers.
Puis la faim qui appelle, afin de tuer la faim
et l'on va se griller le sang, autour des feux.
J'y regarde défiler les passants,
pâle gaieté, éternellement joué
et la voix sur l'épaule:
«las, tu n'es que douteux…»

Once again, it's the sardonic but stubborn
quest, floated along the streets. Pencil, tobacco
and book, the requisite paraphernalia,
until writing wearies, and being alone
with one's own verses.
Then hunger calls, to appease itself,
and I'm drawn to the lights for a bit of warmth.
I watch the pedestrians file by
their washed-out gaiety, eternally played out
and a voice at my shoulder
"but the dubious one is you…"

Que la rue, surtout, soit mon habitante
les vapeurs brûlées des terminus
les pépiements du temps d'orage:
lotissement dans l'été, après-midi lentes
où je vais, prisonnier du chiffre des pas,
voir les péniches disparaître sous les arches
et fumer à l'infini de minces cigarettes
pour accompagner la naissance des vocables.

So let the street be my addiction,
the acrid vapours over the termini
the intermittent spitting of the storm :
the summer's allotment, and slow afternoons
where I walk, trapped in a cipher of footsteps,
to watch the barges disappear under the arches
and smoke my endless, thin cigarettes
to bring these syllables to the surface.

Les deux plis de l'eau contre la pile d'un pont
s'observent mutuellement, en tournoyant.
Au-dessus, de grands pans de ciel d'hiver
comme des glaçons charriés
se cognent et me laissent brisé.
À qui ces bâtisses sourdes, ces encoches
aux façades, et les cris fusant dans les cours?
Paroles de vent que l'inquiétude emporte,
on ne marche pas pieds nus sur le rasoir du jour
que tout aiguise, qu'un rien émousse.

The two crests of water against the pillar of a bridge
observe each other as they divide.
Above, great stretches of winter sky
ferried along like blocks of ice
collide and leave me broken.
Who do they belong to, these sullen hulks, these blind
windows, these cries mingling in the yards ?
Words on the wind, anxiety prevailing,
no one should venture barefoot on the razor's edge of day
that everything sharpens, and anything can blunt.

Poussière d'or, oui, par quel rare soupirail?
Des mains captives et noires
s'agitent dans la pénombre des kiosques
où tremblent les nouvelles du soir.
C'est l'heure, comme on dit, entre chien et loup
entre l'autre et moi, poignée de semblables
qui se heurtent, en pensée, à l'angle des trottoirs.
Le passage d'une pluie d'été, forte à briser
les branches, et la journée tombée ne laissera
que l'ombre d'elle-même à assembler.

Gold dust, coming from the odd basement window.
Hands, dark and constrained
flutter in the gloom of the news-stand
where the evening paper lies trembling.
It is the evening hour, between day and dusk
between self and other, a handful of my familiars
who collide, in thought, at the pavement's edge.
A summer downpour passes over, strong enough
to break branches, and the fallen day leaves nothing
but the shadow of itself to reassemble.

Le passant attardé sur les places ignore
ce qui le porte: le doute, ou le froid
sous les semelles? Paix mal gardée,
demeures en plein ciel. Puis il resserre
de plus près son manteau, à l'idée
des souvenirs, insectes abrités
sous les pierres, qu'il lui faut déranger.
Souvenirs insuffisants, contours tremblés
abri claquant de toiles et de cordes
tout contre le soir près de basculer
– souvenirs de rien, roue cassée.

The passer-by, lingering late in the squares,
cannot tell what drives him on: doubt, or the cold
at his heels? An unsafe security,
dwellings in the open. Then he hugs
his coat about him tighter, at the idea
of memories, insects sheltered
under stones, that have to be disturbed.
Insufficient memories, outlines blurred,
a refuge in the crack of rope and canvas
tensed against the brink of evening
– memories of nothing, a broken wheel.

Pensées de nuit, cailloux au puits
un coup de feu ne les ameuterait pas
ce coup de feu entendu dans les rêves
et dont on se relève sauf, toujours,
et irrémédiablement atteint, au côté.
Le monde a glissé au bord étroit
de la fenêtre – ici, on n'y croit pas.
L'écheveau sans fin plutôt, les mauvais plis
et le corps brûlant de la compagne
qui tressaille et se referme
quand je l'enjambe et me lève sans bruit
– ici, on n'y voit pas.

Night thoughts, handful of pebbles down a well
and gunshot would not rouse them
the gunshot that sounds in dreams
from which one rises safe, always,
and struck, incurably, in the side.
The world has sunk below the narrow ledge
of the window – was it ever there?
The unending tangle, rather, the wrong folds
and the burning body of the woman
who quivers and relaxes
when I step over her and get up in silence
– darkness covers all.

Liasse de l'Est

TROIS MINIATURES

Vent tombé, volets tus, et la lune courant
dans la gaze, prise dans la trame
des nuits anciennes: leçon d'équilibre
contre le nombre et le mouvement.

La geste captive des feuilles, sous le gel:
une dentelle de branches nues et fines,
ossature du ciel, inversant les racines.

Lendemains de neige, les trottoirs encore
scintillants du sel laissé, blanchis
– et reprendre la marche, à perte,
dans la nuit jaune et courbe, soufrée.

East of Here

THREE MINIATURES

Wind stilled, shutters sealed, and the moon riding
in its gauze, caught in the weft
of earlier nights: it's a lesson in balance
against both number and movement.

Leaves trapped under frost:
a lacework of bare thin branches,
bone-work of the sky, roots upended.

Mornings after snow, the pavements still
glittering with salt, scattered, whitened
– we resume the viewless slog into the dark,
crooked, yellow, touched with sulphur.

COMPAGNIES

Avec un ballast neuf, donc gris encore
(ni rougi, ni rouillé ou oxydé, ni noirci)
supportant son poids de neige évaporée
comme les faîtages soutiennent le ciel
ou les canaux leurs reflets de verdures
effrangées; avec les sillons, ornières
de neige, liserons morts, neiges d'hier
et ces plaques blanches sur les hauteurs,
alopécie des collines et des clairières;
avec la campagne décolorée glissant,
courant – au-devant de quoi? Du givre,
du sel, des feuilles captives dans l'eau
durcie, les spectres du froid et de soi.

COMPANIES

With its recent rail ballast, still grey therefore
(and not red, or rust-orange oxide, or black)
bearing its weight of melted snow
rather as roof gables carry the sky
or canals their uneven and greeny
reflections; with ruts and runnels
of snow, dead bindweed, yesterday's snow
and those white scabs on the heights,
alopecia of the hills and clearings ;
with the bleached countryside slipping,
running – away from what? From the frost,
the salt, the leaves imprisoned in iron
water, spectres of the cold, and of the self.

TRAVERSÉES

D'abord, Poix-Saint-Hubert
où un homme seul tanguait
sous les néons de *La Notte*.
Puis Grupont, dont la gare
secondaire ne désirait rien
tant que passer inapercue;
à Forrières, bois d'hiver
entassé le long des rues,
nuancier de mousses et
lichens, avant les églises
de Jemelle, saupoudrées
de poussière. À Marloie,
autres stères, aux bûches
cannelle cette fois; après
Ciney, la ville d'Assesse
que nul ne visite jamais,
et à Courrières (souvenir
de catastrophes minières)
des moignons d'arbustes
sciés sur un talus ébarbé.
À Naninne (ou Louzée?)
des bovins constellaient
les prés en pente, boues
gelées. Après Gembloux,
escarpements, et toitures
effondrées, oui, à Chastre,
à l'image d'un pays entier.

CROSSINGS

First, Poix-Saint-Hubert
where a man was swaying, alone,
beneath the neons of *La Notte*.
Then Grupont, whose station
halt wanted nothing more
than to pass by unnoticed;
at Forrières, winter logs
stacked on roadsides,
colour charts of mosses
and lichens before the churches
of Jemelle, sprinkled
with dust. At Marloie,
more stacked wood, the logs
this time like cinnamon sticks; after
Ciney, the town of Assesse
that no-one ever visits,
and at Courrière (memorials
to mining disasters)
stumps of sawed-down trees
on a cleared bank.
At Naninne (or was it Louzée?)
constellations of cows
on the sloping pastures, mud
frozen. After Gembloux,
escarpments, and yes,
at Chastres, collapsed roofing,
reflecting a whole country.

WAGON DE QUEUE

À travers les deux fenêtres à l'ovale parfait, dans la porte coulissante maintenant scellée comme une iconostase, l'éclat quasi stellaire (rouge, mauve, vert) des sémaphores défilant à quelque cent trente kilomètres heure, allure réglementaire. Pour autant, on ignore ce qui dépose ce film luisant sur les rails (la lune, le néon des gares, des feux de campagne?) dont l'absolue symétrie ne sera pas menacée par les masses de végétation surgies de nulle part, sur des remblais à la mine de plomb: idylle durable, au fusain, entre les viaducs, les passerelles et les lointains, frottés au noir. Et si les voies régulièrement se multiplient (par cinq, dix ou davantage) à l'approche des agglomérations, c'est, dirait-on, pour mieux se contracter ensuite en un système binaire et hypnotique, rivetant l'attention: ce paysage ne déroule-t-il pas, à rebours mais à l'identique, celui que le machiniste voit se jeter sous les roues de la motrice entre signaux, balises et insectes écrasés?

REAR CARRIAGE

Seen through the two perfectly oval windows
set in the sliding door that is now closed off
like an iconostasis, the almost stellar glow
of the beacon-lights (red, mauve, green) races by
at around one hundred and thirty kilometres
an hour, the regulation speed. It is hard to say
what lays that gleaming film along the rails
(the moon, the station's neon, the field fires?)
their symmetry is absolute, unthreatened by
swathes of vegetation springing out of nowhere
and infesting the lead-coloured backfill:
a lasting idyll this, done in charcoal, between
the viaducts, the bridges and the distances,
a smudged-in black. And if the rails multiply
(by five or ten or more) as the built-up areas
approach, it appears to do so the better to retract
into its binary and hypnotic scheme, so riveting
to the gaze. The same landscape, of course,
races by, but reversed, seen by the driver where it
hurls itself under the wheels of the locomotive
between signals, beacon-lights and flattened insects.

CONTRETEMPS

Correspondance manquée, et ce doit être l'inverse de ce qui se produit, dit-on, lors d'une chute depuis un étage élevé: abords ralentis au lieu de l'accéléré entre crissement des rames et wagons manœuvrés, les sempiternelles annonces se succédant dans l'habit d'une voix assurée, les gouttes croisant obliquement l'espace découpé entre les auvents et jusqu'aux flots morcelés, parfois hagards, des voyageurs débouchant sur les quais, histoire de constater ce que chacun sait pourtant: que rien, non, ne brûle autant que le temps lorsqu'il se débite en secondes avant un départ, puis s'étire et renâcle infiniment, en attendant le suivant.

SETBACK

A missed connection, and this must be the reverse
of what happens, supposedly, during a fall from a
high building: a slowing down, not a speeding up,
between the squeal of track and shunted carriage,
the announcements, eternally the same, come garbed
in that smooth voice, the rain slanting down in the
space portioned out between the shelters and the flow,
sporadic, sometimes exhausted, of passengers emerging
onto the platform, and a reminder, as if one needs it,
of how nothing, no, nothing, burns like time when squeezed
into seconds before a departure, and how it stretches out
to infinity, grumbling all the way, in the wait for the next.

CAFÉS DE LA FRONTIÈRE

Il n'y a plus de mines à Volmerange-les-Mines, et plus de cinéma non plus, malgré ce Café du Ciné proposant des chaises où s'asseoir en terrasse, quand le temps le permet. À la sortie du bourg, passé la dernière habitation, le *No man's land* fait face à *L'Entre-Deux*, ex-guérite de douaniers transformée en baraque à frites, de l'autre côté de la route départementale: car la frontière est toute proche, deux cents mètres à peine – et distante de dix années. Je me suis donc arrêté, à cause du nom, tirant ma chaise dans le gravier pour observer la ligne d'ombre qui progressait lentement sur le goudron, hommage subreptice à cet entre-deux auquel je me suis condamné, bronchant entre maintenant et là-bas, entre ici et autrefois, hésitant encore entre moi et moi.

FRONTIER CAFÉS

There are no more mines in Volmerange-les-mines;
no cinema either, despite the Café du Ciné
offering chairs to sit out on the terrace,
weather permitting. On the way out of town,
past the last of the houses, the *No Man's Land*
stands face to face with *L'Entre-Deux*, a former customs hut
now converted into a chip stall on the other side
of the country road: the frontier is close by,
barely two hundred metres
and ten years away. I stopped
because of the name, pulled up a chair in the gravel,
and watched the shadow line stretch
along the tarmac; a quiet homage
to the entre-deux I've sentenced myself to,
stumbling between now and there, between here
and then, still hesitating between me and me.

DERNIÈRE PROMENADE

Onze heures du soir, en juillet, dans la ville
calmée: le bruit des terrasses qu'on range,
des chaises entassées, le cliquetis des chaînes
qu'on cadenasse à l'heure où de vieux chiens
à la démarche empêchée renâclent à rentrer.
Glissent sous les phares façades et carrefours,
aussi vides ou dévastés que le moi aux recoins
familiers, qu'on promène en laisse à son tour
parmi les animaux de compagnie; pour rien,
pour la douceur de l'air et de la température,
pour ajourner l'instant du retour ou encore
parce que, si rencogné qu'il soit, il s'attarde
à ces riens qu'il voit, et dont il a vécu jusque-là.

FINAL STROLL

Eleven at night, July, in the quiet city:
the noise of café terraces being cleared,
chairs stacked up, the click of chains
being padlocked as the old dogs limp over,
hovering at the doorways.
Headlamps slide down shop-fronts, along street corners
empty as the familiar self I'm walking on his leash
among the other domestic animals: for no reason,
for the sweetness of the air, for the temperature,
to delay the moment of return, or perhaps because,
however cornered he may be, he likes to linger
on these nothings that he sees,
and on which he's survived until now.

Neige à Thionville, lumières petites, lumières,
salles à manger, appentis, cuisines éclairées,
maisons basses et jardinets, un instant cachés
par les flancs d'un convoi de la *Transcéréalière*.
Feux mobiles, lancés dans l'obscurité et déjà éteints :
passage sans traces, pour peu que le train accélère
à nouveau et glisse, comme devant, sur les bords
d'une campagne gelée, pour filer une fois encore
vers l'est et le néant, en égrenant sans bruit
les nœuds de l'écheveau.

Snow in Thionville, small lights, lights,
dining-rooms, wallpapers, bright kitchens,
low houses and garden plots, momentarily
hidden by the *Transcéréalière* freight.
Moving lamps, cast into the dark and gone out;
leaving no trace, as the train regathers speed
and slides on ahead through the frozen district
out towards the East and nothingness,
tightening the knotty skein a hitch or two.

La brume a dissimulé la brume qui cache les trois lumières, posées à ras de l'eau, du Café Jean le Pauvre. Du fleuve jauni pendant la nuit dernière, le débit ne cesse plus d'enfler et c'est tout un paysage noyé qui tressaille au passage des trente-neuf (je le sais pour les avoir parfois comptés) wagons des mines, vision pareille et neuve dans le dérèglement continu de la mécanique intime. La part de l'ombre ne se laissera plus, ce soir, apprivoiser: n'importe, sortir et assouplir encore, par un dernier tour, la phrase de peu de secours.

The mist has concealed the mist that hides
the three lights settled on the water's surface
of the Café Jean le Pauvre
The yellow river has swollen in the night,
and now a whole drowned landscape
trembles when the thirty-nine
(I know, I've counted them)
wagons from the mines shunt past,
that same and surprising vision
in the constant disorder of the inner
workings. The dark side shall not, tonight,
be appeased. No matter, go outside, take a last
turn, take the words of small comfort out for a stroll.

Petite ville aux reflets de houille et d'étain,
aux arbres morts plantés vifs sur les remparts,
hautes radiographies de poumons sur fond
de ciel éteint. Et l'on voudrait douter
de ce que l'on voit, comme de la combe
ouverte devant soi, entre les collets posés
des sentiers anciens et les leurres de demain,
au chiffre introuvé. Ne demander qu'un peu
de lumière, de calme intérieur, pour les heures
à venir et la nuit qui suivra: petite loque
de prière serrée entre les dents, gardée.

Small town with its gleams of coal and tin,
its dead trees planted living on the ramparts,
magnified lungs in X-ray on a background
of dull sky. And you would like
not to believe your eyes, or the valley
opened before you, with the traps all in place
along the old ways and the snares ahead
whose number is unknown. Ask for no more
than a bit of light, of inner calm, for the hours
to come and the night to follow: this shred of prayer
clamped between your teeth, and holding.

BALLAST COURANT

Une trainée de cailloux roussis par le soleil
dernier qui tapisse ce soir le mur du fond,
si rarement éclairé, d'une chambre à coucher
entrevue en passant, à l'étage d'un pavillon
d'Uckange ou dans un faubourg frontalier:
dorures fragiles, déjà niellées par un début
d'obscurité avant que ne s'allument plus
loin, sur les façades, les gemmes colorées
des téléviseurs. Pensées de peu, en essaim,
pour aider à traverser le gué des soirées.

SLEEPER GRAVEL

A trail of stones reddened this evening
by the last sun that covers the rarely lit
back wall of a bedroom, glimpsed
on the upper floor of a villa
in Uckange, or a frontier suburb:
fragile goldwork, inlaid already
with the spreading gloom, that interval,
before the coloured gems of TV sets
light the house fronts further on.
Small distracted thoughts, in a swarm,
see us over the gulf of every evening.

CAFÉ DE L'USINE

Usines à froid, usines à chaud, et Grands Bureaux entre Fameck et Hayange. Y tombent à l'oblique, au-dessus des voies ferrées, buses et corbeaux parmi les reliques d'un Noël ancien, ampoules cassées. D'étranges lichens aux teintes soufrées envahissent les terre-pleins sous le ciel normal et bleu, encore tramé par les tuyères abolies des hauts-fourneaux; plus loin, l'usine à rails qui, pour avoir tant dérouillé, peut enfin se laisser rouiller, paisible, dans la campagne recouvrée.

CAFÉ DE L'USINE

Cold steelworks, hot steelworks and Big Offices between Fameck and Hayange. Slanting down above the rail-tracks come crows and buzzard among the relics of a Christmas past, smashed fairy-lights. Strange sulphurous-tinted lichen invades the embankments under the untroubled blue sky, still criss-crossed with the disaffected blast-pipes of the furnaces; further off the rail-forging factory, having done so much work unrusting can now, in peace at last where the country has resumed, rust over.

FÉVRIER

Neige éparse distraite, à peine
lestée du poids de l'air lui-même
parmi le volettement des odeurs
de givre et d'industrie ancienne.
Feuilles remuées dans les angles
morts comme coques d'insectes
séchés, terre gelée et dimanche
dormant, assiégé par les freux,
à tisonner entre cendres et feu.

FEBRUARY

Sparse and scattered snow, barely
weighing more than the air itself
with its cross-flitter of smells,
antiquated industry and frost.
Stirrings of leaves in the dead
corners like dessicated insect
shells, earth hard-frozen and Sunday
asleep, besieged by the rooks,
a stoking between ashes and fire.

PAVILLON DES INCURABLES

Nous aurons quand même eu, pour finir, ces belles après-midi de juillet puis d'août, aux heures si lentes à passer sous les feuillages vernissés de la cour Gamard (*Heu mortis fortasse tuae quam prospicis hora*) avec leurs fondrières au repos et leurs souvenirs raccrochés, anciens, mais encore à portée de ta main dont les doigts s'agitaient, désignaient, conversaient presque, sur le drap jaune estampillé *Hôpitaux de Paris*.

De temps à autre, la porte du couloir s'entrebâillait et tu ouvrais pareillement les yeux, curiosité salutaire, sur l'infirmière qui s'approchait pour les mesures d'usage: pouls, tension, température, histoire d'être sûre que le corps tiendra jusqu'à la prochaine visite.

D'autres fois tes pensées glissaient en terrain inconnu d'où tu ramenais d'étranges phrases désarticulées mais non sans beauté – tu te reprenais d'ailleurs aussitôt et t'empressais, en t'excusant, de corriger.

Un soir, ils t'ont transporté dans une autre chambre plus spacieuse, d'où tu aurais presque pu apercevoir le bras nu qui, périodiquement, sortait d'une fenêtre le temps d'une cigarette, le clocheton de zinc ajouré à l'angle d'un toit, les festons d'une façade éclairée dans la rue de Sèvres (ou était-ce la rue Vaneau?) et les feuilles écartées, à cinq doigts, d'un marronnier que l'été commençait tout juste d'oxyder, devant la stèle obscure de la tour Montparnasse fichée dans un ciel bleu-noir. «Je suis une piètre compagnie...» disais-tu encore, et aucune n'aurait pu être plus précieuse lorsque tu somnolais, puis rouvrais les yeux, étonné d'être là, avant de redemander à boire (l'haleine de la nuit d'août, entre les battements du store).

HOSPICE WING

We were after all granted, in the end, those fine
July, then August, afternoons; their slow hours
spent beneath the shiny leaves of the Cour Gamard
(*Heu mortis fortasse tuae quam prospicis hora*),
our talk falling silent then jump-started
here and there by old memories, but still within reach
of your hand, whose fingers fidgeted, pointed things out, conversed
almost, against the yellow monogrammed *Hôpitaux de Paris* sheet.
From time to time, the door into the hallway creaked open
and your eyes opened in the same vein – such heartening curiosity –
upon the nurse coming by on her rounds:
pulse, blood pressure, temperature, making sure
the body would hold until the next visit.
At other times your thoughts slid into unknown territory
from which you brought back strange dismembered sentences,
though not without beauty – you'd immediately catch yourself
anyway, apologise, and quickly correct them.
One night they took you to another room,
more spacious, from which you could almost see
the naked arm from time to time emerging from a window
long enough for a cigarette, the zinc turret open
on a sloping roof, the decorative uplit façade
of Rue de Sèvres (or was it Rue Vaneau?),
and the five spread-fingered leaves of a chestnut tree
that the summer had just begun to rust
facing the dark tombstone of Montparnasse Tower
skewering a blue-black sky.
'I'm such poor company', you kept saying,
though none could have been more precious to me
than when you dozed, then opened your eyes, surprised
to be here, before asking for a drink (the breath
of an August night between the flapping blinds).

Ton front à rafraîchir, le pistolet à rincer, tes lèvres
à humecter, petits gestes mécaniques pour que cette
dernière semaine s'égoutte, elle aussi, sans peine.
Le décompte, commencé en mille neuf cent dix sept,
s'est achevé un mercredi, vers six heures du soir:
la morphine aidant, tu es parti sans trop souffrir
et peut-être (je me le demande encore) sans savoir.

Forehead to be dabbed, bedpan to be rinsed, lips to be moistened – little mechanical actions to help whittle down that final week, so that it passed, it too, painlessly. The countdown, begun in nineteen-seventeen ended one Wednesday afternoon, around six in the evening: accompanied by the morphine, you left without suffering too much and maybe (I'm still wondering) without knowing.

Sous le crible

LES MAUVAISES SOIRÉES

autrement dit où l'on ne sort guère de soi
et encore moins de chez soi, dans le seul
véhicule d'une paire de sandales fanées
pour arpenter le territoire et ses confins,
reprendre l'un ou l'autre livre en main
sans en élire aucun, tâcher de combler
les retards du courrier puis y renoncer
quelques lignes plus loin – en résumé,
où l'on renâcle, insatisfait, à mi-chemin
entre faim et satiété, incapable pourtant
de nommer cela qui persiste à manquer.
Des phrases ou bris de vers affleurent ici
et là, qui ne laisseront que leurs miettes
à ramasser, comme brins de tabac guidés
du tranchant de la main vers la corbeille
à papier. Et la pensée se berce dans ce va-
et-vient, tâtonne vers son nadir jusqu'à
ce que l'heure nous enjoigne de dormir
– et de se débarrasser enfin des sandales
sans âge: les idées, aussitôt, s'allègent,
grimpent à l'assaut d'abrupts raidillons
puis s'égaillent par des sentiers volages.
La soirée, finalement, n'était pas si ratée;
mieux, on se surprend même à souhaiter
qu'elles puissent toutes lui ressembler:
ne finirait-on pas, tôt ou tard, par avancer?

Under the Sieve

THE BAD EVENINGS

by which I mean those when you scarcely
venture out of the self let alone the house,
with nothing to carry you over the territory
and its limits but a pair of faded sandals;
when you pick up one or other of the books
on the go without choosing either, or try
to catch up on some correspondence before
giving up after a few lines – those, in short,
when you balk, dissatisfied, somewhere
between hunger and repleteness, yet unable
to identify what, exactly, is still missing.
Sentences or spars of verse surface here
and there, and leave nothing but their shavings
to be gathered like strands of tobacco, guided
towards the waste-paper basket with the edge
of the hand. Your thought is coddled in this
coming and going, and feels towards its nadir,
until the hour enjoins you to go to bed
– and to shed those old sandals; which done,
your ideas lighten up suddenly, and tackle
steep slopes, then scatter along heady paths.
The evening was not, in the end, a write-off;
better still, you even surprise yourself wishing
they would all be like this: sooner or later
you are sure to make some progress, who knows?

UN GESTE

infime et ancien, que celui consistant à appuyer le dos de la cuillère tout contre le bord du bol ou de l'assiette à soupe pour empêcher celle-ci de goutter sur le trajet de la bouche; rite sonore, à peine, lesté par une longue pratique dans l'enclos de cuisines trop ou mal éclairées, dans le périmètre des campagnes sourdes ou banlieues verticales, à l'écart: geste de femme ou d'homme seuls sous le plafonnier, de pensées ralenties revenant buter sur l'obstacle de penser quand la main, suivant la courbe, s'abaisse un peu vers la fin, dans l'assentiment d'exister.

A MOVEMENT

tiny and venerable, consists in running the back of the spoon
over and against the edge of the plate or soup-bowl
to stop it from dripping on its journey to the mouth;
a rite, faintly audible, and worn through by long
practice in over or under-lit narrow kitchens,
within the confines of a one-eyed village or a vertical
suburb, left to themselves; an action that belongs
to a lonely man or woman, under a bare bulb, thoughts slowed,
returning to stumble against the obstacle of thinking
when the hand, following the curve, drops a little,
right at the end, as it re-acknowledges existence.

NOËL À ITHAQUE

Malgré la barque illuminée, tirée hier sur la place, et les réverbères décorés (à raison d'un sur quatre, sur la jetée) de guirlandes intermittentes, un seul battant aura finalement fait résonner le métal de la Nativité. Rues d'Eumée, du Cheval de Troie ou de Télémaque: sur les cartes au fond bleuté, Ithaque a la forme d'un sac plié ou tournoient les courants d'air, au milieu étranglé par un lacet invisible, trois fois noué.

CHRISTMAS ON ITHACA

Despite the illuminated boat, drawn up
yesterday in the square, and the lamp-posts
decorated (one in every four, on the jetty,)
with lights blinking on and off, a single slamming
metal shutter is what ushers in the Nativity.
Eumaeus Street, Trojan Horse Street,
Telemachus Street: on the blue-backed
maps of Ithaca, the island looks like
a folded knapsack around which turn
the winds, strangled in its middle
by an invisible thread, knotted thrice.

ENCORE

À la fin on se lasse de l'odeur poivrée
des moquettes dans les escaliers d'hôtel,
de la lanière des soirs entaillant l'épaule
et des couloirs humides longés sous le vent
entre des façades qu'on ne reconnaît pas.
Et le moindre pavé descellé sous la semelle
manque de faire basculer le monde au-dedans
et ses quelques lumières éparses, devant.

ONCE AGAIN

By the end you're tired of the peppery smell
of hotel staircase carpeting,
of those evenings strapped to your shoulders
as you lounge along damp corridors in the wind
between shop-fronts you don't recognise.
And the slightest uneven flagstone underfoot
threatens to bring the world crashing down inside you
and the few scattered lights ahead.

EXIT

Dernières soirées et dimanche en creux près du *Kladaradatsch!*, où l'heure grise étire les passants du boulevard Anspach, entre les ruines des chantiers et la brique des pignons, dans les couloirs d'une ville qui se sera peu éclairée, mais où luisent parfois les filins d'acier, à la géométrie parfaite, de deux paires de rails tendus vers des quartiers de l'âme mal connus.

EXIT

Last few evenings here, plus a hollow Sunday
near the *Kladaradatsch!*, where the grey hour
draws the passer-by on Boulevard Anspach
between the ruins of the roadworks and the redbrick
gables of the houses, through the corridors of a city
that's barely lit but where there sometimes glitters
the perfect geometry of steel threads: two pairs of rails
stretching towards the unknown corners of the soul.

3H56

Dans le bruyant convoi de Porto à Salamanca
traverser à la sauvette un chapelet de gares
en veilleuse, et trop promptes à nommer
la campagne accroupie dans l'obscurité;
puis le paysage ralentit avant la frontière,
s'immobilise en grinçant pour laisser monter
l'éternel passager, à l'arcade sourcilière
béante sous le sang séché, qui se cherchera
longtemps une place parmi les corps endormis
et bien décidés à le rester. Et le wagon
tout entier sent l'oignon entamé, le tabac
refroidi et les conversations inachevées
cependant que nul ne voit, dans le jour
débutant, le relief lentement changer,
la bruyère supplanter la vigne, et les bordées
d'eucalyptus se raréfier sur les côtés.
Et l'on devient soi-même, encore une fois,
un autre – à quoi bon, sinon, voyager? –
et celui qui déjà nous attend à l'arrivée.

3.56 A.M.

In the noisy convoy from Porto to Salamanca
slicing through a line of dozing stations, too fast
to see their names, the countryside
cowers in the darkness;
then the landscape slows before the frontier,
scrapes to a high-pitched halt to let on
the eternal last passenger, a deep cut to his eyebrow
under a crust of dried blood, who shuffles
for a space among the sleeping bodies
determined to remain so. The whole carriage
smells of chewed onion, cold tobacco, unfinished small-talk,
and meanwhile no-one sees, in the emerging day,
the heather supplanting the vine, the eucalyptus
borders thinning out along the hills.
Once again you are becoming that someone else
– why bother travelling otherwise? –
already awaiting your arrival.

LA MATINÉE DES CHOSES INSIGNIFIANTES

où j'aurai croisé tour à tour le regard d'une femme s'égosillant dans un portable («Non, je ne peux pas vous le passer, il est en visite sur un chantier...»), un facteur en tournée poussant son chariot jaune vif en compagnie de sa fiancée, un homme écrasé par sa songerie derrière la vitrine d'une cafétéria d'hypermarché (aussi pimpante, m'a-t-il semblé, qu'une cantine des impôts ou qu'un self d'usine), avant de remarquer dans un bus la poignée d'une béquille équipée d'un cataphote, comme un vélo, deux locomotives accolées en une étreinte canine, combien d'autres saynètes entre-temps disparues – et reconnaître au retour ce bruit très familier de machine à laver dans la cage d'escalier: tous événements miniatures confirmant la précieuse, ancienne et taraudante appartenance à la tribu.

THE MORNING OF INSIGNIFICANT THINGS

in which one by one I caught the eye of a woman
shouting herself hoarse into a mobile phone ('No I can't
fetch him for you, he's out on a building site...'),
a postman on his rounds pushing his bright yellow
trolley accompanied by his fiancée, a man crushed
beneath his thoughts behind the window of a hypermarket
cafeteria (as brightly-polished, it seemed to me,
as a tax-office canteen or a factory self-service),
before noticing, on a bus, the handle of a crutch
equipped, like a bike, with a reflector;
then two locomotives rutting like dogs...
and how many other little dramas forgotten since?
Then recognising, on my return, the familiar sound
of washing machines in stairwells: those miniature
happenings there to confirm our precious
ancient and stubborn belonging to the tribe.

EN TRAIN, POUR CHANGER

Cela n'aura duré qu'un instant, il y a moins d'une minute de cela, le temps d'entrevoir un incendie de fanes ou herbes sèches entre deux voies, et les copieuses fumées bleutées qui s'en échappaient en tourbillonnant: là, derrière ce rideau (dans son entrebâillement, plutôt) est apparu un troupeau de ruminants dociles, puis un fuyant alignement de pylônes électriques et les unités perdues d'une armée en déroute – celle des ballots de foin éparpillés sur un flanc de coteau. (Il ne fallait pas vouloir rouvrir ce carnet, chercher un bic, car la vision aura bien sûr entre-temps disparu, de cet Eden mi-rural, mi-industriel, et très hypothétique.)

ON THE TRAIN (FOR A CHANGE)

It only lasted a moment, less than a minute
all in all, just long enough to notice
a brush-fire or some hay being burned
between two tracks, the copious blueish smoke
rising in swirls: and there, behind this veil (or rather
in its parting) appeared a herd of docile
cattle, then a disappearing fractal of electric
pylons and the abandoned units
of a routed haybale-army, scattered
along the slope. (Lucky I didn't open
this notebook and look around for a pen,
because the vision would surely have disappeared
in the interim, this semi-rural
semi-industrial, and very hypothetical Eden.)

CELA

aurait pu débuter, une fin septembre, par de larges traînées roses dans un ciel partagé par les squelettes des grues dressées dans le quartier, en perpétuelle reconstruction, de la gare du Midi, se poursuivre ensuite dans un restaurant camerounais, *Le Vieux Mila*, de la rue de Moscou, le temps de voir inhumer à la télévision les morts non réclamés de la canicule dans le coin dit des indigents du cimetière de Thiais, puis d'assister sous un ciel new-yorkais aux épisodes d'un match de tennis – combat de rétiaires protégés durant les pauses par de jeunes porteurs d'ombrelles empruntés au siècle d'Hérode – avant de se terminer, tard dans la soirée, sur un long monologue échappé d'une fenêtre ouverte à proximité de l'hôtel. Cela, ou la vacuité légèrement déhanchée d'un dimanche s'interrogeant sur son emploi du temps, à l'étranger.

IT

might have started one late September, with long
pink streaks in a sky partitioned by the skeletons
of cranes above the perpetual building site
of Gare du Midi; it may also have continued
in a Cameroonian restaurant, *Le Vieux Mila*,
on Rue de Moscou, just long enough to watch
the unclaimed dead from the heatwave
buried in the so-called 'local' section of Thiais cemetery;
prolonged itself by watching, under a New York sky, a few episodes
of a tennis match – gladiators face to face across a net,
shaded in the breaks by young parasol-bearers from Herod's time –
before finishing, late at night, with a long monologue
rising from an open window near the hotel. That
or the faintly unmoored emptiness of a Sunday
as you wonder how to spend your time
when you're abroad.

ODE (POUR TRAVERSER LES JOURS SANS MAUGRÉER)

à la petite tasse émaillée, au rebord bleuté, dont le métal brûle lorsque, par distraction, on la saisit non par l'anse, mais par les côtés. Compagne des débuts de nuit et des travaux en cours, jamais très éloignée du *Nouveau dictionnaire analogique* de Niobey sur quoi il lui arrive d'être posée – et qui veille seule au milieu des objets, à la température exacte de la pièce, avant de resservir le lendemain et les lendemains des lendemains, intacte.

ODE (FOR GETTING THROUGH THE DAYS WITHOUT WHINGING)

to the little enamel cup, with the blue-tinted edge
and the metal that burns, if you seize it
distractedly by the sides and not the handle.
Companion of the night-shift, of the works
in progress, never too far from the Niobey
Nouveau dictionnaire analogique on which
it is sometimes placed – it sits on alone
amongst the objects, at the exact temperature
of the room, before being used next morning,
and the morning after the morning after, intact.

Décembres

Voici plusieurs jours, en somme, que j'observe dans un rayon variable, qui va de l'encadrement de la fenêtre aux grands axes et ruelles alentour, la réinstallation des guirlandes dans les arbres, sur les grues, les façades, sans pouvoir congédier l'impression très tenace qu'il s'agit là de tessons pour la vue, d'angles vifs et blessants dans le noir prégnant, de barbelés lumineux en quelque sorte, aussi peu faits pour allumer l'idée d'une fête au-dessus des passants qu'un morceau de corde posé sur la table d'un pendu récent. (J'exagère, sûrement; il n'empêche, comment désactiver pour soi-même cette électricité veuve, aux entrelacs clignotants?)

Decembers

For several days now, in short, I have observed
in a varying arc reaching from the window frame
to the major axes and the tributary streets
the redecoration of the trees with Christmas wreaths,
on the cranes and on the house fronts, unable to expunge
the tenacious impression that these are so many
shards on which the gaze will wound itself, like so much
luminous barbed wire scarifying the dark, as apt
to inspire the idea of festival as a piece of rope
placed on the table of a man just hanged. (I exaggerate,
I know, but how can I turn off, for myself,
this bereaved voltage with its flashing intervals?)

Décembre, mois entre tous malcommode
à dire, à raison de ce qu'il célèbre, exhibe
en le cachant, tient enfoui sous l'enfance
et ses âges, entre potlatch et renoncement.
D'où, sans doute, ce presque soulagement
de l'heure première, à l'instant de quitter
la nuitée intime et ses amonts incertains,
pour une aube extérieure balisée de lueurs,
réverbères, trottoirs vivants. La journée,
au su et au vu de tous, aiguise ses pointes
et ses stylets, ou bien dispose ses édredons,
plis d'oreiller, nuages courbes, c'est selon.

December, month the most awkward of all
to describe, because of what it celebrates,
and exhibits by hiding, buried beneath
childhood and its revisitings, between potlatch
and renunciation. Which is where this quasi-
appeasement comes from, at first light,
emerging from the close dark with its
unsteady currents into a dawn swept by lights,
streetlamps, living streets. The day now
fully in the open sharpens its spikes
and knives, or disposes its eiderdowns
and pillows, its curved clouds, depending.

Veille de veille de Noël dans l'Est, cette année encore, et repas de fête annoncé à la brasserie de la place Wallis, qui offre quelques chambres en étage à de jeunes émigrées russes en transit: le 24 décembre à 20 heures, *Traïpen mat Äppel (boudin aux pommes)* et vin mousseux; la télé, continûment branchée sur un canal animalier, y déroulera pour rien des reportages nombreux sur les mœurs des hyènes, la toilette des grands félins, la chasse à l'éléphant ou le déplacement des oursins. En regard de la place, pour animer le tableau, La Maison du Diabète, une taverne de l'Aiglon à l'enseigne désuète et, contrastant avec la boutique de régime voisine, les néons du cabaret Coyote Girls pourvoyant à l'envi promesses de spectacles et de divertissement.

Antepenultimate day before Christmas in the East, yes, this year too, and a feast is announced in the Brasserie of the Place Wallis, which has a few rooms to let for young Russian emigrées in transit. 24th December at 8pm Traipen mat Äppel and sparkling wine; the TV is fixed on a wildlife channel broadcasting uninterruptedly the habits of hyenas, the cleaning rituals of the great cats, elephant hunting or the movement of bear-cubs. Enlivening the scene, there's the Maison du Diabète opposite, a tavern under the quaint sign of the Aiglon, and oddly coupled with the diet shop next door the neon lights of the Coyote Girls cabaret, peddling shows and entertainments a go-go.

Par la fenêtre un petit homme en cache-col bronze et chapeau de feutre grisâtre, flanqué d'un quadrupède au poil plus miel que roux, et qui escorte chacun de ses pas. L'étonnant est que tous les deux s'immobilisent parfois longuement malgré le froid, pour ausculter le ciel ou en dévisager les abords immédiats, regardant passer les voitures et les suivant des yeux jusqu'au tournant, puis pivotant de trois-quarts pour jouir d'un autre angle de vue, avant – à l'issue d'une station plus longue encore que d'habitude (admirable patience du chien, qui feint de s'intéresser aussi à ce presque rien dont il est témoin) – de se résigner à rentrer, à pas prudents que le verglas étrécit. Et quand on les croit disparus, ils sont là de nouveau, en faction, l'homme au couvre-chef gris et son renard miniature au poil plus blond que roux, qui emboîte chaque demi-pas de son compagnon.

Through the window a little man in a bronze scarf
and a grey felt hat is flanked by a quadruped
more honey-coloured than russet, who escorts
his every step. The astonishing thing is how
the two of them stop dead sometimes, for long
intervals, and in spite of the cold, to scrutinise
the heavens or their immediate surroundings,
watching the cars go by until they reach the corner,
and then the two of them swivel three-quarters round
to enjoy a further view before – emerging from a longer
freeze even than usual (wonderful patience of the dog,
who pretends to take an interest in the quasi
non-events he witnesses) – they resolve to go home,
footsteps reduced by the ice. And when you think
they've gone, there they are again, in league,
the man with the grey hat, and the miniature fox,
with a coat more blond than russet, who follows
in his companion's every semi-footstep.

Arrière-cour en hiver, avec fumées montant droites contre un ciel couleur chair, et clartés tamisées sur les façades voisines, sans aucun des tressautements colorés par les téléviseurs: le lait de cette Nativité n'en sera pas tourné. Une soirée tranquille, en somme, pour relire Cendrars, Strindberg, ou quelque prosateur d'Europe centrale à peu près ignoré. La neige tombée hier sur le balcon s'est recroquevillée avec d'infimes crissements (mais quel travail du gel saura tenir compagnie en suffisance?). Un rectangle d'étoiles se déplace de guingois entre les toitures, flocons de sel sur du papier huilé, à la trajectoire millimétrée: une bonace nocturne, pour ainsi dire, nimbant sans effort le mobilier perché des antennes et cheminées. L'inquiétude est, pour l'heure, lac peu visible d'ici, à la surface sombre et qui ne tremble pas.

A closed courtyard in winter, smoke climbing
straight up against a flesh-coloured sky, and gleams
filtered onto the facing walls, with none
of that flickering colour from televisions:
this Nativity's milk will not be turned by them.
A quiet evening, in fact, on which to re-read
Cendrars, or Strindberg, or some quasi-unknown
Central European proser. Yesterday's snow
on the balcony has contracted in a series of tiny
crackles and fizzes (but how hard must it freeze
to sound, well, companionable?) A crooked rectangle
of stars has come down between the roofs, flecks
of salt on oil-coated paper, traced to the nearest
millimetre : a nocturnal lull, shall we say, halo-ing
the rooftop furniture of aerials and chimneypots.
For now, anxiety is a lake, scarcely visible
from here, with a dark, untrembling surface.

La saison se désincarcère de la saison, à reculons, les traînées de sel semblent maintenant l'emporter en quantité sur la neige lorsque celle-ci, devenue motteuse et grisâtre, s'efforce malgré tout de durer dans l'air adouci, en monticules ternes et racornis qui rappelleraient assez des cadavres de hérissons. Ou bien s'aplatit à l'écart en plaques goudronnées, par l'ombre sauvées; quelques jours après la chute, les derniers cristaux encore immaculés sont ceux qu'on aperçoit sous les algues, à l'étal des écaillers – et qu'ils s'apprêtent à jeter au caniveau, une fois les festivités passées.

Grudgingly, the season cuts free from the season,
and trails of salt now dominate in quantity the snow
even though the latter all packed and grey tries to hang on
in the softer air, in dull, hard little mounds that bring
to mind if anything dead hedgehogs. Or else it is
flattened in asphalted sheets, preserved by shadow.
A few days after the fall, the last immaculate crystals
are the ones below the seaweed, on the shellfish stall
– and about to be dumped into the gutter, once
the partying is over.

Le Train des jours

GRUES ET FUMÉES

Visibles ce matin de la fenêtre comme chaque matin, quelques ouvriers en tenue orange, casqués, occupés à démouler, étage après étage, l'immeuble neuf qui s'élèvera bientôt à la place de l'ancien cinéma Victory, détruit. À mi-distance, tendue sous un auvent de zinc branlant, et remuant tout juste sous les coups de vent, une serviette couleur bleu roi, évoquant assez une toile de Thomas Jones intitulée, si je ne me trompe pas, *Un mur à Naples*; et une volute de fumée s'échappant avec un débit variable d'un conduit parallélépipédique débouchant, rouge brique, parmi des toitures en pente. Voici donc pour les choses aperçues en mouvement aujourd'hui: le gris d'une fumée, un menu rectangle bleuté et les déplacements huilés, tout à fait silencieux, de deux grues jumelles détourant leurs armatures jaunes contre le ciel brouillé – sans oublier les blocs de béton énormes dont elles sont lestées, et qu'il est impossible de ne pas imaginer chutant au milieu des passants, ou sur des carrosseries de voitures aussi faciles à froisser que du papier aluminium entre les doigts d'un marmiton. Grues et fumées: elles me paraissent assez bien figurer, tandis que je les observe alternativement, deux principes qui nous sont, d'une certaine manière, inhérents: le dur et le gazeux, le rigide et le volatil, le solide et l'inconstant, autrement dit le jaune et le blanc, l'eau et le fer, la plume dans le vent et ce qui a été bâti pour lui résister sans plier. Ou encore la nuée, la buée, les vapeurs, les exhalaisons

Days Going By

CRANES AND SMOKE

Visible this morning through the window, like every morning, a group of labourers in hard-hats and orange overalls, engaged in freeing, like a multi-storied cake from its mould, the brand new tower-block, rising where the old Victory cinema used to be, now gone. In the middle distance, spread out below an unsteady zinc awning, and stirring very slightly in the gusts of wind, a royal-blue towel, that strongly brings to mind a painting by Thomas Jones entitled, if I'm not mistaken, *A Wall in Naples*. There's a scroll of smoke of variable outflow escaping from a parallelepiped conduit, poking up from amongst the angled roofs. This, then, is the gist of things perceived to be in movement today: grey smoke, a small blue rectangle, and the well-oiled, absolutely silent movements of two twin cranes, whose yellow armature is thrown into relief against the clotted sky – not forgetting their attachments, two huge blocks of concrete ballast, whose only-too-imaginable-fall would scrumple the cars below like a sheet of tinfoil between the hands of a baker's boy. Cranes and smoke: observing the one and then the other, they seem to figure twin principles, both of them in some sense intrinsic to us: the hard and the vaporous, the rigid and the volatile, the solid and the flighty; or in other words yellow and white, iron and water, the feather in the wind, and the thing constructed to resist the wind unyieldingly. Cloud and breath, condensations

et, d'un autre côté, la mécanique engrenée, faite maison. Les unes et les autres montrant d'ailleurs une résistance analogue, survivant aux saisons et au bal des semaines, guère menacées dans leur existence et peu menaçantes. Grues et fumées aux mouvements gratuits ou calculés, compagnie accoutumée de jours, comme elles, partagés entre la construction et la déperdition, entre le ciment et la dissolution: double exemple à suivre, absolument.

and exhalations, and against them, the home-grown machinery with its cogs meshed. Both principles, what's more, exhibit a similar kind of resistance, to the seasons and the weekly cycle, their existence on the whole unthreatened and unthreatening. Cranes and smoke, with their movements random or calculated, habitual accompaniment to days that are, like them, divided between building and dispersal, cementing and coming loose, both after their fashion exemplary, and hence to be followed.

MI-AOÛT FERROVIAIRE

Après les soubassements en grès rose de la gare de Thionville, et cette mention en relief, Hayange, tout juste visible sur le flanc des rails, grande vitesse en direction de Bordeaux Saint-Jean, cependant que la rame accolée poursuivra vers Hendaye. Et la canicule de regrouper tous les passagers sous les auvents des quais, comme chèvres crétoises à l'ombre d'un bosquet, et une femme en noir de s'éventer avec son billet en attendant quel prochain départ? Quinze août: on doit s'éventer de même dans chaque bar – et sur les lits superposés, dans les cellules de la maison d'arrêt de Gradignan.

ENTRAININGS, MID-AUGUST

After the pink stoneware platforming of Thionville
Gare, and the stamped legend, Hayange, just visible
on the side of the rails, this then is the grande vitesse
to Bordeaux Saint-Jean, coupled from behind
by another TGV that will carry on towards Hendaye.
And the dog-day heat herds all the passengers
under the platform shelters, like Cretan goats
in the shadow of a bosky grove, and a woman
in black fans herself with her ticket, waiting for
some further departure. Quinze août: there's fanning
going on, even in the bars – and on the bunk-beds
in the cells of the prison-house at Gradignan.

Marmande, 22h30: train annoncé avec un retard de soixante minutes à destination d'Agen, Montauban, Toulouse, Nîmes, Montpellier et Marseille. Et donc tout le temps de détailler mes voisines, deux dames conversant sur un banc latté, ou le jeune père («Au revoir, oui, embrasse les enfants…») manipulant à n'en plus finir son téléphone portable, dans le gigantesque courant d'air d'un train annoncé sans arrêt par une sonnerie aigrelette et une voix d'homme à l'accent gascon, nous invitant à nous éloigner de la bordure du quai. «À la mémoire de Laguerre François, agent de la SNCF tué par fait de guerre 1939-1945», non loin de la terrible affiche des disparus (depuis tant d'années, pour certains, qu'il a fallu les vieillir artificiellement): Denise Pipitone, Léo Balley, Jerôme Cautet, Yannis Moré, Marion Wagon. L'air aura imperceptiblement fraîchi pendant cette attente aux secondes énumérées par un chien muselé et haletant, ou par quelques grillons officiant de l'autre côté des voies.

22.30, Marmande: the train for Agen, Montauban, Toulouse, Nîmes, Montpellier and Marseilles will be sixty minutes late. So plenty of time to observe my neighbours, two women chatting on a slatted bench, or the young father ("Good bye, yes, and kiss the children...") toying unceasingly with his mobile phone, in the colossal whoosh of air that comes in the wake of a non-stop train announced by falsetto siren and a male voice with an accent from Gascony, inviting us to keep clear of the edge of the platform. "To the Memory of Laguerre François, employee of the SNCF, killed in the war 1939-1945", near the terrible poster of the missing (and missing for so long, some of them, they've been artificially aged): Denise Pipitone, Léo Balley, Jérôme Cautet, Yannis Moré, Marion Wagon. The air has grown imperceptibly cooler during the wait, every second counted out by the muzzled, panting dog, and a few crickets, officiating, the other side of the tracks.

Une fois à bord du train enfin arrivé, et aussitôt lancé à l'assaut de ses freinages à venir, entre crissements variables et ronflement équanime («Toulouse Matabiau», *Toulouse-Tue-Bœuf* traduit-on dans un demi-sommeil) sur les couchettes de ces trains corail d'autrefois, avec savon à molette dans le cabinet de toilette et drap glissant sur le skaï des banquettes: qu'a-t-on vu, et su, et retenu pendant toutes ces années où l'on s'apprenait à voyager? Question à se reposer quelques heures plus tard, sur les marches de l'escalier de la gare Saint-Charles, dans l'agitation disparate des aubes déplacées: Hôtel Grenoble-Savoie, Hôtel de France, chaises en osier tressé, terrasses, premier café – ou les termes d'une équation très peu assurée, celle de la monade en mouvement pour qui l'avenir signifierait tout, moins le passé et son présent.

Safe now aboard the train, no sooner arrived than hurled
into the breach of fresh brakings, screechings that vary
the steady snoring rhythm, ('Toulouse-Matabiau', whose
translation, *Toulouse-Kill-Bull*, comes to the passenger
half asleep) – and travelling couchette, the slippery surface
and the sliding sheet, and in the cabinet de toilette the soap
on its crick, features of the old express train: so what sights,
what knowledge, from all the years spent learning to travel?
Something to be asked a few hours later, on the steps
of the Gare Saint-Charles, in the disparate turbulence
of misplaced dawns: Hôtel Grenoble-Savoie, Hôtel de France,
the cane chairs, café terraces, the first *serré* – the terms,
in fact, of a very uncertain equation – the monad in movement –
for whom the future means all, less the past and its present.

Notes in Transit
(Le Train des jours, 2013)

Breakfast at the *Florida*, on Place du Capitole in Toulouse, after a night spent in an overheated compartment, slid between two empty couchettes like one slice of ham between two of bread, negotiating a contract with sleep whose terms will finally only be honoured an hour or two before we arrive, while the rosary of ghost towns tells itself outside. Their names will have left no more trace than those of rare vineyards murmured into the ear of a teetotaller.

Between movement and immobility, which to choose? The immobility of movement, brought home to us by short train journeys, or the movement of immobility, or rather its inner jolts, its intimate spasms, which perhaps find their order later on, like early childhood memories that hung on a few names or placenames, and even then barely hung at all. In the train from Strasbourg to Metz, this morning: a moment of absolute attentiveness to the world – ending in a sort of gradual retraction, in a form of absence, of withdrawal, a retreat into something a little beyond the world. Three cows upright for every seventeen lying down, all of them optically distorted through the glass of these carriages that could themselves be from another era: the straightness of the rails transforms into vermicelli that fluctuate in proportion to the fixity of the oak sleepers beneath them, horizontally wedged into the ballast that holds their decimetres of cast-iron fittings. Then a brutal return to reality as I peruse, along one of the platforms at Thionville station, two worn posters, worded with a sort of tamped-down dread:

The lost children
Do not forget them

Yannis More, born 13 May 1986, went missing 20 May in Ganagobie – image computer aged

Elisabeth Brichet, born 30 August 1977, went missing 20 December 1989 in Namur – image computer aged

On to Marseille. Passing through the station at Brunoy, which triggers a fleeting memory of Henri Thomas, who shared an apartment here with Kenneth White – before the train lunges through fields of pylons, channel-hopping as it were, through Burgundy, then slows down on the approach to Avignon, and the sight of a beige Renault 4 parked beneath a shrub.

The 8.26 stopping train. – Platform 1 for Saint-Charles was in places completely black from the falling fruit of a wild blackberry bush. A stamp, *Lorraine Escaut*, seen on the side of a rail lit from the side, and then another miniature journey: Port de Bouc, with its canal, its faraway boats and its red and white striped chimneys, then Croix Sainte, in the middle of the countryside – two disused platforms sidling up to another canal (or is it the same one?), so darkly green it looks black and oily. Then Martigues, invisible, with its clouds shredding themselves across the overpass, and industrial (so to speak) quantities of tank cars, before La Couronne-Caro with its shaking foliage, then Sausset-les-Pins and its mastless sail-boats, pulled up ashore or left in gardens, in the same sidelong light even though the angle it now falls at has imperceptibly changed, and Carry le Rouet with its laundry drying on clothes-lines, shaken as much as the branches above by gusts of twisting wind. At La Redonne-Ensues, with its little ravines below, there's a little pleasure port where you can almost hear the masts clicking in the endless white puffs of cumulus, then at last Niolon at L'Estaque, as the local capital approaches, settles down among sterile fig trees and shards of jagged broken glass that flash (always in that same sidelong light) along the crests of the security walls.

From Morhange to Morenges. Finally, finally… as soon as we leave Metz station, the time comes to enjoy watching the train choose another route, try a different journey, cut through other fields. 'Rail journeys remain the best things we've ever invented to chase away the blues' (Roger Rudigoz). All the better if it's to launch ourselves into the blue, leaden epicentre of an oncoming storm that's ready to lash the windows and which, even now, transforms the needles of crashing water into a miniature diaparous rainbow. A passenger lifts her frightened eyes from the grid of her crossword, shaken, excited and delighted by the sudden violence of the rain against the moving train. For most of this journey, my neighbour's crutch has been playing footsie with me, so to speak, while its owner has been canoodling (there's no other word for it) with her mobile phone.

Mid-August: it's the time of the year when the bales of straw start to sag under their own weight and under the weight of the weeks that have passed inside them; it looks as if they have seeped into soft ground. And then: hangars, silos, a few burly, not to say lumbering, pylons, stiletto-sharp belfries, the geometric perfection of the maize fields motionless under their brownish rustle and that perpetually desolate sight of sunflowers sagging on their stalks, water towers and farms…

all in all just what you'd expect from the working countryside. Reassuring.

On the way into every large or even medium-sized town (Saverne, Strasbourg, Sélestat, Colmar, Mulhouse), comes the inevitable parade of little gardens with sheds displaying their hollyhocks, climbers and fruit-bushes, all of which precede by a few minutes the usual suburbs, the usual variety of *Ibis* and *Etap'hôtels*, empty stadia, warehouses, railway wastelands – all the sights that presage the arrival of a city. In Colmar, where the opening of the doors coincides with a blast of continental heat, I noticed a new kind of railway sleeper, looking more like metallic dumbbells, concreted down at each end and surely designed to replace, one day, their solid oak counterparts, which sweat in the heat and bead up with a sort of perpetually tarry resin. And at Saint Louis, last stop before Basel of the two stations, the train lingers inexplicably, so there's all the time in the world to watch a small emaciated-looking gang of youths crack open their umpteenth can of beer, then to compare the floral arrangements in their ornamental tubs, and then cast an eye over a few grassy weeds, piercing, here and there, the asphalt coating of the platform. It occurs to me that these clandestine plants, fragile and disdained, at the mercy of any old foot – plants that don't officially exist – aren't so far after all from providing us with a serviceable yet absolute definition of beauty.

Removals
(Carnets de ronde, 2004)

Out of the depths of these weeks, barely or poorly lit, which signalled, nonetheless, the presence of an even darker place, where eye and mind settled assiduously on the flame of the unknown soldier flickering on the far side of a bridge resting on gouty piles ; during these nights overlit by the orange sodium from a streetlamp placed right in front of the window, so powerful that on snowy evenings it shone through the flakes until I could believe (and not for the first time) that I was trapped in one of those plastic paperweights shaken into a whirl of artificial snow. If I wanted, I could read without switching on the lamp.

In the neighbourhood: an Armenian news-seller, as reserved as his wife – in compensation – is smiley; a sex shop announcing 3000 programmes to choose from and three specialities that light up the night in yellow letters on a red background (*Leder, Lack, Latex* – if I can moreorless visualize the business with leather and latex – the *Lack* option remains intriguing); I have never seen anyone emerge except, one afternoon, looking quite relaxed, one pale blond labrador; two seamstresses (*Maxi-retouches*, and a newcomer, *Family retouche*, that must be resented by *Maxi-Retouche*); a watch-and jewellery shop almost always empty; a hairdresser called Fernand, a shop, condemned by its own desuetude, *Electro-Viaduc*, and a *pastificio bolognese*. Of good repute.

Getting used to new noises: the tapping of heels

above, the sound of the door below, the piano next door, the blinds opposite, the shouts escaping from a nearby gym at the end of the day. Moving from flat to flat, from area to area, is a way of outwitting the different stories of the self.

Refusing to 'settle down', one spends one's entire time doing just that, 'settling down'.

And still suffer from the vulnerabilty of the dislodged hermit crab. No progress in that direction, one never hardens up. At the most one just perfects the art of filling boxes with books that pile up in the rooms to be left, the old and the new landings, and the new rooms. An existence packed, stocked, and carted about, countable in boxes.

Postcard-view: the milky block of a bank, the lit-up letters of the Hôtel Cravat (at first I saw *gravat* – the Hotel Rubble), a cathedral with three spires, the curved bridge crossed by small silhouettes à la Marquet, at every hour of the day; in the foreground the imagined yappings of a dog stuck in front of a pedestrian crossing, the orange brazier of workmen across from it, a line of streetlamps with their sulphurous halo, and the fog, taking its shortcut, drowning everything out.

Visible in the disordered gloom of the house (the new one) after the fuses went: gaping boxes, books lying loose, a disgorging of objects, the open guts of a removal. A precise photograph of a life, its order gone missing.

From a rear window, I can see the façade of a building that turns out to be the top police HQ (done out in the exact colours of a two-scoop ice-cream, strawberry on the façade, and vanilla on the window surrounds), and whose occupants, when they regain their cars parked in the courtyard at the end of the day, trigger spotlights as powerful as an interrogator's lamp. A century earlier, no doubt the same men would have emerged, in cloak or frock coat, to hail a carriage or signal to a coachman.

February: the sky is yellow before it snows, padded pink when it is snowing, and opaque white after it has snowed.

And all of the tiny objects (broken toys, packaging, nappies, clothes-pins etc.) fallen off balconies and scattered on the top of the glass-ceilinged sealed-in veranda that now serves as a courtyard – solid little gobs, spat out by daily life and its inhabitants.

From one morning to the next, passing below the window, juggernauts with identical markings on the side: *Wallenborn, GoodYear (Mehr Kilometer pro Reifen!), Schneider & Schneider Spediteure, Rentz logistic S.A.*; they resemble commuters on wheels. There are also cement mixers striped lengthwise, like pyjamas or Obelix's pantaloons, buses with spaniel ears, pastille-coloured ambulances. Visions, in short, to occupy the weeks that lie ahead.

The evening lull. The traffic has thinned a bit. The silhouette of a young woman crosses the bridge, hurrying home, holding a plastic bag that must contain shopping for her dinner. The startling clarity of lights sliding across the tarmac gleams like a stretch of river. As if one's vision had suddenly cleared, or been cleansed. To be where one is, and not elsewhere, from now on to see what one sees and not something else: there is no more to it, in fact, than acquiring the habit. And so return to the flickering flame above the Unknown Soldier, as to a constant beacon, a lantern in the distance. Come spring, the foliage might conceal it.

Change of Address

*from the Alzette, lentil green or brown
according to hour and season, with its
talkative ducks quacking through nights
on the Grund, to an avenue with doorways
blackened by car exhaust, encircled by
the lava flow of their tail-lights. Whatever,
(as they say).* Sic transit. *We're moving on.*

Notes in February
(La Nuit de Moyeuvre, 2000)

An isolated quotation, penned in a margin: 'The writer's best work, and it is the same with any craftsman, comes once the first weariness has been overcome.' My poem on Hagondange would be an example of this: I have never written it, even though every time I pass the place on the train its ghost or the desire to write of it revives, but this is as quickly discouraged by my incapacity to describe the dullness of the place. Which in turn is to ask, once more, the age-old question: is the lack primarily mine, which is then imposed, forcibly, on a landscape that is not to blame but still... or does it indeed emanate from the sight of those over-straight main streets and the adjoining suburbs with their shuttered windows, which transmits lassitude to the eye regarding it, without its knowledge? (One day, though, I shall get off at Hagondange, and I shall walk up the main street long enough to approach the idea of what I had come for, before turning back, and taking refuge in the only restaurant open near the station, Au Pavillon d'Alsace, where for forty-nine francs drink included I can regale myself with a sclerotic-looking choucroute. And the bread will taste a tad acidic in the basket as they unroll the green baize in the public bar, and a retired unionist will sing out 'Bonjour, belle enfant!' in reply to the 'Salut, Lucien!' proffered by the amenable, over-blonde waitress, and a ray of light, as if refracted through stained glass, will strike my beer mug, and then I shall be able to say that, for an instant, the lack is indeed in the eye that observes and not in the object observed.)

AFTERWORD

Few writers convey, as deeply and as recurringly as Gilles Ortlieb, the sense of being at once anchored in a place and utterly estranged from it. As with place, so with time: caught between the fleeting and the static, Ortlieb deals in the in-between: between stations, between hotel rooms, between departure and arrival, between a now that refuses to take shape and a then, whether behind or up ahead, that is too nebulous to fix upon. It's what he calls, in 'Frontier Cafés', 'the *entre-deux* I've sentenced myself to':

> stumbling between now and there, between here
> and then, still hesitating between me and me.

Trains, hotels: that's the title of a section of *Place au cirque*, Ortlieb's 2002 volume of poems. And what is more 'in-between' than those two modes of – how to describe them? – staying and going? Of staying and going *at the same time*, in the same movement, in the same absence of movement? In the hotel you are moving in a still place; in a train you are still in a moving place. Gilles Ortlieb has both bases covered.

At the level of form, the in-between-ness of Ortlieb's states and places is echoed in and prolonged by the relationship between the poem and the note, the volume of verse and the carnet or the notebook. The two have been dancing so closely for so long in Ortlieb's writing that often they become one: the poem inhabits the page with its justified right-hand margin like a *bloc* of notes, as if resisting – modestly but firmly, and out of respect for its material too – the kind of devices, the pretentions, the *éclat* and the prestige, that being a 'poem' would force upon it. In parallel, the notes themselves, gathered in books like

Vraquier (literally a bulk carrier or a freighter), *Sous le crible* (Under the Sieve), *Le Train des jours* (Days Going By), have the rhythm and the aerated quality of prose poetry or even free verse.

Ortlieb has himself remarked that everything in his work begins in note form in the *carnet*, and the poem as such is the note taken up a gear. It customarily undergoes a formal change which is made manifest in the margins, left justified and right justified (or as near as humanly or mechanically possible). The original notebook entry undergoes thereby a tightening, an ingathering, a condensation, but it is not changed in kind. Regarding the poems, the translator must take care to preserve the block-like consistency of construction, the solid object made of minute noticings, that singularly Ortliebian paradox. The poet has throughout his writing life played with that frontier between writing that asserts itself as poetry and writing that wants to retain the unmediatedness as well as the immediacy of the *carnet* or the logbook. This is poetry that is true to its materials, to borrow from the language of architects, that pays its dues to its origins as notes and observations, as lines of scattered prose or as meticulous descriptions of everyday things.

Ortlieb calls the note / poem border a *frontière*, but he knows too that frontiers are constructs, and they are there to be crossed, blurred or erased. It is therefore appropriate that so much of Ortlieb's poetry and prose has been located on – over? across? along? – frontiers: the Belgian-French-Luxembourg-German borders, where he spent a large part of his working life. His territories are the French and Belgian Lorraine, Luxembourg's industrial heartlands, the agro-industrial Gaume and Ardennes of Belgium. This is where his writing is so characteristically itself: in those industrial and post-industrial landscapes, bypassed as much by literature as by economists and politicians, where countries and languages overlap and bleed into each other. Ortlieb writes of the 'mix of affection and lassitude' for these places, and adds: 'tempered nonetheless by a debt of gratitude for these landscapes which offer what they can.' *They offer what they can*, they *do their best*, and we are grateful in turn to Gilles Ortlieb for giving them their place in literature.

*

Having observed the work develop over a long period – over forty years – is to appreciate the way its successive sedimentations have suddenly, viewed now from further off, formed a surface solidity, an entire stonescape that is as imposing as it is unbreakable. The writerly choices adhered to early on and retained throughout, which at times looked like 'scrupulous meanness' taken to an extreme, are revealed as an entire way of seeing, or *noticing*, possessing its own consistency and logic.

A typical Ortlieb text (poem or prose) is frequently a 'scoop', into and out of what is immediately there around the poet. But there exist more elaborated pieces, in which a process of distillation (the French have the word *alambiqué*) has clearly followed upon the initial scoop. 'Cranes and Smoke', for instance, requires a particular discipline on the part of the translator who must as far as possible respect the line-lengths, measured not in stresses or syllables but in centimetres – ie dictated by the margins, justified left and as near as possible right as well.

If there is the visual requirement of replicated line length in poems like 'Cranes and Smoke' or

'Entrainings, Mid-August', there is an equivalent phonic requirement as well. There is a restrained but audible harmony, and a measure of musical resolution to be found in these poems, generated by the traditional resources of alliteration and assonance, inflections that work like handholds or steps, running up and down the sheer block of the text. Again, the translator is called upon to achieve an echoing musicality, something which, mercifully, is afforded by the resources of the target language. If Ortlieb's texts do on occasion offer satisfactions to his English translators, it is because his work belongs more with the 'hard' type in French poetry, to reuse Pound's distinction, rather than to the school of the 'soft', the purveyors of silk and talcum: there is about him more of Corbière than Verlaine.

He almost marries the two schools, though, in the memorable names, Hayange, Uckange, Hagondange and the rest. These place names, evocative of the industrial past of the now stricken Lorraine, amount to 'found poems' which Gilles Ortlieb has lighted upon and appropriated. The poem 'Crossings', made up almost entirely of names, is a veritable phonetic homage to *la Belgitude*.

Salient features of Ortlieb's style also include the wholesale importation of street signs, memorials, the names of bars and brasseries and cafés and shops and cinemas: just as Monet mixed in sand – the grit of the real or real grit – into his collages so this poet imports the street directly into his writings. There is an entire poetics in these lines:

> Then recognising, on my return, the familiar sound
> of washing machines in stairwells: those miniature
> happenings there to confirm our precious
> ancient and stubborn belonging to the tribe.

As translators we have throughout *The Day's Ration* respected the acoustic, place-specific nomenclature. Though how specific really is it? Frequently the names seem plastered on, and the *Etap'* hotels or the *Ibis* are in any case part of a chain. They are clumsy or lazy imports themselves. Gilles Ortlieb dislikes symmetries, and he notices (with grim approval) how the fittings in a cheap hotel room, the stains, cracks, warps, things crooked and awry, don't... *fit*. There is always the choice, to transpose or domesticate, to use the jargon, but that would be to falsify the topography and the detailing. In the notebook prose proper names tend to proliferate: 'two seamstresses (*Maxi-retouches*, and a newcomer, *Family retouche*, that must be resented by *Maxi-Retouche*)', and the listing is often, as here, steered by a guiding hand and a wry humour.

Patrick McGuinness &
Stephen Romer

ACKNOWLEDGEMENTS

Grateful acknowledgement is made to the French publishers of Gilles Ortlieb who have facilitated the publication of this volume: François Boddaert of Éditions Obsidiane, Georges Monti of Éditions Le temps qu'il fait and Thierry and Emmanuelle Boizet of Éditions Finitude. We are also grateful to © Éditions Gallimard for permission to reprint poems from *Place au cirque* (2002).

Some of these poems (in translation) first appeared in the following UK journals and anthologies: *Modern Poetry in Translation, Poetry Review, Times Literary Supplement, High Window, Twentieth-century French Poems*, ed. Stephen Romer, (Faber 2002); *Into the Deep Street: Seven Modern French Poets 1938-2008*, ed. Jennie Feldman & Stephen Romer, (Anvil Press, 2009); *Writing the Real*, ed. Nina Parish & Emma Wagstaff, (Enitharmon, 2017); *French Poetry: From Medieval to Modern Times*, ed. Patrick McGuinness, (Everyman Pocket Library, 2017); *A New Divan*, ed. Barbara Schwepke & Bill Swainson, (Gingko Library, 2019).

BIOGRAPHICAL NOTES

GILLES ORTLIEB was born in Morocco in 1953. He returned to France in the 1960s where he studied Classics at the Sorbonne, before switching to modern Greek. At this period he travelled widely in the Mediterranean, with a predilection for Greece. In 1986 he moved to Luxembourg, where for many years he worked in the translation service of the EU.

He has published over thirty books, ranging from collections of poems and notebooks to an account of Baudelaire in Belgium (*Au Grand Miroir*, 2005), two volumes of critical essays, and a prize-winning meditation on the post-industrial landscape of Lorraine, *Tombeau des anges* (2011). A prolific translator from modern Greek (Solomos, Cavafy, Valtinos), he is currently at work on a multi-volume translation of the diaries of George Seferis, to be published by Éditions le Bruit du temps.

PATRICK MCGUINNESS is a poet, novelist, and translator. His latest collection of poems is *Blood Feather* (Jonathan Cape, 2023). His first novel, *The Last Hundred Days*, appeared in 2011. His second novel, *Throw Me to the Wolves* (Cape, 2019), was followed by a personal account of the city of Oxford, *Real Oxford* (Seren, 2021). For Arc publications he has translated Hélène Dorion's *Seizing : Places* (2012) and *Europe in Poems: The Versopolis Anthology* (2020). He is Professor of French and Comparative Literature at Oxford, and a Fellow of Saint Anne's College.

STEPHEN ROMER is a poet, critic, editor and anthologist. His latest collections include *Set Thy Love in Order: New & Selected Poems* (Carcanet, 2017) and a French bi-lingual collection *Le fauteuil jaune* (Le Bruit du temps, 2021). He has edited two anthologies of French poetry, *Twentieth-century French Poems* (Faber, 2002) and (with Jennie Feldman) *Into the Deep Street: Seven Modern French Poets, 1938-2008* (Anvil Press, 2009). His anthology *French Decadent Tales* was published by Oxford World Classics in 2013. He is Lecturer in French at Brasenose College, Oxford.

SEAN O'BRIEN's poetry has received numerous awards, including the T. S. Eliot Prize, the Forward Prize, the E. M. Forster Award and the Roehampton Poetry Prize. His most recent collection of poems, *Embark*, appeared in 2022, and his *Collected Poems* in 2012. His fiction includes the novels *Once Again Assembled Here* and *Afterlife*. He is also a critic, editor, translator, playwright and broadcaster. Born in London, he grew up in Hull. He is Professor Emeritus of Creative Writing at Newcastle University and a Fellow of the Royal Society of Literature.